for beginners

Agile Coaching for Beginners

Guide and Support Agile Teams in Implementing Agile Principles and Practices for Improved Performance

Printed in the United States of America

First Edition: 2025

www.littlebiggiant.com

Introduction

The meeting room smells like burnt coffee and stuck ideas. A whiteboard is full of sticky notes that nobody can read. People circle a table and speak over one another. A junior developer taps a pen, voice small: "What if this fails?" The question lands like a stone. Faces go quiet. The project timer shows another week missed. On the wall, a small poster reads Agile Coaching for Beginners. Nearby, a printed note says Guide and Support Agile Teams in Implementing Agile Principles and Practices for Improved Performance. A known fact hangs in the air too: the Agile Manifesto was written in 2001 by 17 software developers. That manifesto did not hand teams a map. It handed them four values and a lot of questions. Teams learned the hard way that ideas need practice. Coaches began to appear to help teams turn those values into work that actually moves.

Someone clears a throat. A coach walks to the whiteboard and points to one sticky note. The coach asks one short question and the room leans in. The question is simple, almost too small to matter. It promises a way out, but it also asks everyone to try something different. Hands twitch. A senior developer looks afraid and excited at the same time. There is warmth in the room now, like a small light under a door. The clock keeps ticking. This moment could change how the whole team works, or it could be another effort that collapses. Who will take the first tiny step? What will happen when that step is taken?

Table of Contents

Chapter 1

Introduction to Agile Coaching

By the end of this chapter you will understand the role and value of an agile coach, the core agile principles, and how coaching differs from mentoring, teaching, and managing.

Defining the role and value of an agile coach

You are a guide, not a boss. An agile coach helps a team see its own path, choose good next steps, and learn how to work better together. You ask questions, listen carefully, and help the team find the answers that fit their situation. You help the team decide how they will work, what to improve, and how to measure progress. This is not about giving orders; it's about unlocking the team's ability to learn and adapt.

Think of a coach as a steady hand that helps a group stay focused on goals while staying flexible about how to reach them. You help create a safe space where ideas can be shared, mistakes can be examined without blame, and small tests can be run to see what works. The value you bring shows up in three big ways.

First, you improve communication. You design conversations so everyone's voice is heard, especially quieter team members who might hesitate to speak up. You encourage clarifying questions, active listening, and constructive feedback. Second, you accelerate learning. When a team hits a rough patch, you help them see patterns, surface assumptions, and try quick experiments that reveal what actually helps. Third, you increase reliability. By guiding the team to agree on small, testable steps, you reduce guesswork and make progress visible sooner.

In real teams, the agile coach often works with several people at once: developers, testers, product owners, and sometimes stakeholders outside the team. You don't own the goals; you help the team own them. You don't decide the plan; you help the team discover a plan that makes sense to them. You don't do the work for them; you enable them to do the work better, faster, and with less drama.

Two short, practical examples help show how this works in practice.

Example one: A new team keeps arguing about priorities and feels stuck. You sit down with the team and ask simple questions: "What does the customer want most this week? What would make the customer's life easier in the next two days? If we tried one small change, what would we check to know if it helped?" The team drafts one small experiment—perhaps prioritizing one story and showing it to a user for quick feedback. After the experiment, you help the team review what happened, decide what to try next, and keep the loop short.

Example two: A team has trouble with handoffs between developers and testers. You facilitate a short retrospective to surface the friction and then propose a tiny change, like pairing or a one-hour joint review. The goal is not perfection but learning: did the change help the team flow better this week?

If yes, keep it; if not, adjust. The point is to keep trying small, observable changes and learn from each result.

In both cases you remain focused on what the team can do itself. You model how to ask powerful questions, how to listen deeply, and how to keep the conversation moving toward concrete steps. You also protect the team from external noise—unnecessary meetings, conflicting demands, or sudden shifts in scope—so they can stay focused on what matters most.

A quick note on boundaries: you are not a manager who assigns tasks and tracks people. You are a facilitator who helps people choose tasks, align on goals, and own the outcomes. You are not a trainer who pours in a fixed curriculum; you're a partner who helps the team discover the best path for their own context. And you are not a critic who points out faults; you are a coach who helps the team learn from every action, whether it works or it doesn't.

To remember your value in everyday work, practice two habits. First, pause before you give advice. Ask, "What would the team like to try first?" Second, celebrate learning, not just results. When a plan doesn't go as expected, name the learning clearly and decide the next small test together.

Core agile principles and the mindset shift required

Agile coaching rests on a few core ideas that guide every choice you make with a team. You don't need to memorize every rule; you need a working understanding of the shifts that make agile real in practice. Here are some principles expressed in plain language, followed by the mindset shifts that support them.

First principle: people and collaboration are more important than rigid processes or heavy tools. Agile teams thrive when people talk openly, share knowledge, and help each other. You support collaboration by creating spaces for equal participation, encouraging dialogue, and reducing barriers that keep people from contributing.

Mindset shift: let curiosity lead. Instead of prescribing a perfect sequence of steps, you ask: "What will make collaboration easier here?" You look for opportunities to bring people together, not to push a single way of working.

Second principle: deliver value early and often, not after long, perfect planning. Teams should produce tangible outcomes regularly, learn from feedback, and adapt.

Mindset shift: embrace incremental progress. You encourage the team to break work into smaller pieces, test them quickly, and measure what actually helps the customer. Small, visible wins beat big, unseen promises.

Third principle: transparency and inspection matter. When work is visible and feedback is frequent, teams learn faster and adjust sooner.

Mindset shift: make learning visible. You model openness—show how plans change, how decisions are revisited, and how data from experiments informs next steps. You help the team build a culture where it's safe to say, "That didn't work," and then try something different.

Fourth principle: respond to change over following a fixed plan. When new information appears, the best move is often to adjust course rather than stubbornly sticking to the original plan.

Mindset shift: treat change as information, not as failure. You guide the team to reframe changes as clues about what customers actually need, and you help them use those clues to improve quickly.

A few practical steps to embody these principles day to day:

- Ask open questions that reveal the real needs behind a problem. Questions like, "What would success look like this week?" or "What are we learning from this? How will we know if it's true?" keep conversations constructive.

- Create rituals that expose learning. Short experiments, frequent demos, and quick retrospectives help the team see progress and learn from failure without blame.

- Keep work visible. A simple board, a shared backlog, or a live progress update helps everyone see what's happening and where to help.

- Protect learning time. Guard against unnecessary meetings or last-minute scope changes that steal focus from experimentation and reflection.

Two concrete micro-cases highlight how these principles show up in practice.

Micro-case one: A team is anxious about deadlines and feels pressed for time. You help them reframe the work into a series of small, testable outcomes. They run a one-week experiment to deliver a minimal viable feature and gather quick user feedback. The feedback becomes the compass for what to build next, not a pressure that forces rushed decisions.

Micro-case two: Product owners want a long, detailed plan for the next six months. You facilitate a shift to shorter cycles, with a clear cadence for planning, delivering, and reviewing. The team learns to adjust the plan after each cycle, using actual results rather than forecasts alone to guide choices. Over time, the plan becomes a living document that changes as learning grows.

These principles are not rules to memorize; they are practices you bring to life through your daily actions. You model the behavior you want to see: curiosity, collaboration, honesty about what's known and what isn't, and a bias toward learning over proving.

Distinguishing coaching from mentoring, teaching, and managing

Coaching, mentoring, teaching, and managing are different ways of helping others grow. They are tools in a toolbox, and you will use them at different times. Here's how to tell them apart in practical terms.

Coaching: you help people think for themselves and grow their capability. You ask questions, listen carefully, and guide discussions toward outcomes. You don't give step-by-step instructions for every situation. You help the team design its own path and build the skills to keep going after you're done.

Mentoring: you share personal experience and knowledge to help someone grow. Mentors offer guidance based on their own paths, often focusing on career development, specific skills, or industry wisdom. Mentoring can be ongoing and more directive because it relies on the mentor's experience.

Teaching: you transfer knowledge through content delivery—lectures, demonstrations, or training sessions. Teaching is often planned and structured to convey a topic or method. It can be very useful for building a shared base of skills, but it is mostly one-way.

Managing: you assign tasks, set expectations, track progress, and hold people accountable for outputs. Management is about control and coordination of work, ensuring people complete what was planned, sometimes with less emphasis on how they learn or adapt.

Two quick scenarios to illustrate:

Scenario A: A team is stuck on a difficult technical problem. If you act as a coach, you ask questions to surface assumptions, help the team test small ideas, and guide them to choose their own solution. If you instead teach, you present a method or a known fix for similar problems and walk the team through it step by step. If you mentor, you might share your past experiences dealing with a similar problem to give guidance. If you manage, you assign someone to fix it and track progress.

Scenario B: A junior developer asks for a skill you already know well. If you coach, you design a safe practice together, then let the developer try and reflect. If you teach, you give them a clear lesson plan with new material. If you mentor, you might share your personal journey of learning that skill and offer tips. If you manage, you assign a task tied to a broader project timeline.

How you choose the right approach depends on the goal, the context, and the person you're working with. In many cases, you blend methods. You coach to grow capability, mentor to share experience when it's valuable, teach to build a shared skill set, and, when needed, help with coordination and outcomes in the mold of management.

As you practice, your aim is to be clear about your role in each moment. You want to be helpful without taking over, guiding without dictating, and enabling without becoming a bottleneck. If you sense the team feels you're stepping into a control role, step back and reframe: ask a question, invite a suggestion, or propose a small experiment and let the team own the next move.

Key Takeaway: A successful agile coach unlocks a team's own problem-solving power by guiding with questions, protecting learning time, and helping the group turn insight into action.

Coming up next: Core Agile Frameworks and Practices – comparing Scrum, Kanban, and Extreme Programming at a glance; essential practices like iterations, backlog refinement, and WIP limits; and guidance on when to adopt, adapt, or blend frameworks. This next chapter will show you how to translate the coaching mindset into concrete ways teams organize work and flow, so you can start applying what you've learned here to real team needs.

Chapter 2

Core Agile Frameworks and Practices

1) Comparing Scrum, Kanban, and Extreme Programming at a glance

You have three common ways teams organize work, and each one hangs on a different idea about how to move tasks from start to done. Scrum emphasizes a steady rhythm of planned work.

Kanban emphasizes smooth flow and visibility. Extreme Programming, or XP, emphasizes the engineering practices that keep code clean, reliable, and easy to change. Understanding these differences helps you pick the path that fits your team's situation, or mix them in safe, practical ways.

Scrum gives you a timeboxed rhythm. A sprint is a fixed period, usually one to four weeks, when the team pulls a set of tasks from a backlog and works to deliver a usable increment of the product. You run planning at the start, daily check-ins, a review at the end, and a retrospective to learn what to improve next. The core idea is to create predictable cadences you can measure and improve. In a classroom or club project, Scrum helps you schedule progress, define what "done" looks like, and regularly check in with a stakeholding audience, whether that audience is a teacher, a parent, or teammates.

Kanban flips the cadence idea on its head. There isn't necessarily a fixed sprint. Instead, work flows from one state to another on a board. Columns show stages such as To Do, In Progress, and Done, and cards move through those columns as work progresses. The key guardrail is WIP—work-in-progress—limits. If you cap how many items can be in progress at once, you reduce bottlenecks, force focus, and speed up overall throughput. Kanban works well when work arrives irregularly or when you want to keep continuous delivery without waiting for the next sprint. It also helps teams that must support ongoing operations while still delivering new features.

Extreme Programming, XP, centers on the engineering discipline behind the product. It pushes practices that improve code quality and adaptability: test-driven development (writing tests before code), pair programming (two people at one workstation to share eyes and ideas), continuous integration (integrating changes frequently), refactoring (keeping code clean as it grows), simple design, and customer involvement to ensure the product stays aligned with real needs. XP isn't just a process; it's a way to make software more reliable in the face of changing requirements. If your project asks for frequent code changes and you care deeply about quality, XP practices can be layered into other frameworks to strengthen the technical backbone.

Two short micro-cases illustrate how these approaches look in action. Case A drops you into a small school project that uses Kanban. The team sets up a board with columns labeled Backlog, In Progress, Review, and Done. Each member pulls the next item when they have capacity, and they set WIP limits—no more than three items in progress at any time. They can spot bottlenecks quickly: if “In Progress” fills up, they know to either help each other or move some items back to Backlog to keep the line moving. Results show a steady flow of completed tasks, fewer context switches, and clearer visibility for teachers who want to track progress.

Case B puts you in a software club using Scrum. The team agrees on two-week sprints, with a planning session at the start to decide which tasks will be finished, a daily stand-up to keep everyone aligned, a sprint review to demo what's built, and a retrospective to identify improvements. They build a small feature each sprint and can forecast delivery more reliably. The cadence helps with collaboration and accountability, and it creates natural points for feedback from a real user or stakeholder.

Case C blends XP with a Scrum-like cycle. The team uses short development cycles, emphasizes automated tests, and practices continuous integration. They still hold sprint-like planning and reviews, but the emphasis on engineering quality means more time is spent on refactoring and test coverage. The result is code that's easier to extend and adapt, with bugs caught earlier because tests and quick feedback are built into the process.

These examples aren't rules carved in concrete. They're patterns you can adopt or adapt, depending on what your team needs. The main takeaway is this: Scrum gives you discipline and predictability; Kanban gives you flow and visibility; XP gives you the engineering discipline that makes growth and change less painful. You can keep one framework as your backbone and borrow successful ideas from the others, as long as you keep communication clear and flows steady.

2) Essential practices: iterations, backlog refinement, and WIP limits

Iterations (timeboxed work cycles)

Iterative work means you break work into regular, repeatable periods. In many teams, this is a sprint or a fixed planning window. The idea is simple: you choose a set of outcomes you want to deliver within that window, you commit to finishing them, and you review what you've done when the window closes. Timeboxing creates a predictable rhythm you can measure, compare, and improve. It also helps you gather feedback in a timely way, so you're not waiting months to learn what works.

To apply iterations well, start with a clearly defined goal for each period. Decide what "done" means in practical terms, not just a vague wish. Keep the window fairly short—one to two weeks is a good starting point for many teams—so you can learn quickly and adjust. At the end of each period, hold a brief review with stakeholders to confirm what's ready and what might need adjustment. The retrospective—yes, a small, honest debrief—helps you identify one or two concrete improvements for the next cycle.

Backlog refinement (grooming)

Backlog refinement is the regular practice of revisiting the list of work that could be done, making it clearer and more ready to pull in a future iteration. In plain terms, you take vague ideas and turn them into well-defined tasks with acceptance criteria so you know when they're complete. The goal is to have a healthy backlog that's easy to navigate, with items that are well understood, appropriately sized, and prioritized.

How to refine well: set a recurring time, even if it's short, to review items. Ask questions like: Is this worth doing? What does "done" look like for this item? How big is this item? What will be the first step? Make sure each item has a simple description, a rough estimate, and clear acceptance criteria. Keep it practical; you don't need perfect specs for every task, just enough clarity to move forward when it's chosen for a future iteration. Regular refinement reduces surprise and makes planning faster and more accurate.

WIP limits (work-in-progress limits)

WIP limits are guardrails that cap how many tasks can be in a certain state at the same time. The purpose is to prevent people from juggling too many things at once, which often causes context switching, delays, and lower quality. When you set a WIP limit, you force the team to finish or move along existing work before taking on new items. This tends to smooth the flow, shorten cycle times, and reveal bottlenecks sooner.

Putting WIP limits into practice is straightforward. Start with a modest cap, like two or three items per person or per workflow stage, and adjust based on how the team feels and what the data shows. Watch for stuck work or long queues in any column. If work piles up in a particular stage, you may need to add capacity there, rework the process, or refine items to be smaller and clearer. The key is to treat WIP limits as living guidelines, not rigid cages. They're there to help you move faster, not to punish slow progress.

Two micro-cases help ground these ideas. In Case A, a group using Kanban with WIP limits discovers that too many small tasks are leaving the "In Progress" column at once. They reduce the limit, and suddenly people focus on finishing what they started. The flow improves, queuing drops, and the team finishes more items per week. In Case B, a Scrum team uses timeboxing and backlog refinement to keep sprints realistic. They double-check estimates, rewrite vague stories, and prune tasks that would cause scope creep. With clearer scope, the team delivers more consistently and spends less time chasing after surprises.

3) When to adopt, adapt, or combine frameworks

Sometimes you start with one framework because it's the simplest thing to do, and that's okay. What matters is recognizing when to adopt, adapt, or blend ideas from different frameworks to fit what your team needs now.

When to adopt a framework as-is

Choose Scrum if your work benefits from regular planning, concrete commitments, and routine feedback. If your environment has new or uncertain requirements, the sprint cycle helps you learn and adjust in small, visible steps. Choose Kanban if your work arrives in an ongoing stream, you want to optimize flow, and you prefer a lightweight planning rhythm without fixed sprint boundaries. XP is a better fit when you're building software or products that require high quality and frequent changes; if you can support rigorous testing, refactoring, and collaboration, XP practices can dramatically improve resilience.

When to adapt the framework

Most teams don't stay perfectly within one framework. You can adapt by borrowing the best pieces from another approach. For example, you might run Scrum sprints but use Kanban-style workflow boards to visualize work, or maintain fixed iterations while applying XP practices like automated testing and continuous integration to keep quality high. Adaptation helps you tailor the rhythm and practices to how your team actually works, rather than forcing a textbook method that feels foreign.

When to blend and hybridize

A blended approach—sometimes called Scrumban or XP-Scrum—lets you mix the predictability of Scrum with the flow of Kanban and the engineering discipline of XP. You might plan in sprints, but also run a continuous improvement heartbeat with a Kanban board showing work in progress. Or you might hold pair programming sessions and automated testing within a Scrum sprint to lift technical quality without sacrificing cadence. The goal is to keep the team productive and focused on outcomes, while continually improving how you work.

Two concise examples illustrate blending ideas in practice. Example 1 uses a Scrum backbone with a Kanban overlay: sprints provide planning and review, but the board with WIP limits helps the team see bottlenecks and slow down to finish what's in progress. This keeps momentum while preventing overload. Example 2 fuses XP with Scrum in a new product effort: you keep short planning cycles and stakeholder reviews, but you lock in automated tests and frequent integration to maintain high-quality code as features expand rapidly. The result is a predictable delivery rhythm that still keeps the codebase healthy and adaptable.

Key Takeaway: Start with a rhythm that fits your team's needs, then borrow ideas from other frameworks to improve flow, visibility, and quality. You can grow toward a tailored blend that keeps delivery steady and learning constant.

Coming up next Subtittle: Building High-Performing Teams

1) Stages of team development and targeted coaching actions,

2) Fostering psychological safety and trust to enable risk-taking,

3) Encouraging cross-functionality and collective ownership

Chapter 3

Building High-Performing Teams

By the end of this chapter you will know how to guide a team through its development stages, create psychological safety, and foster cross-functional ownership so they can work together with real commitment.

Stages of Team Development and Targeted Coaching Actions

You start by recognizing where your team sits on the classic path of forming, storming, norming, and performing. Each stage has its own needs, and your coaching actions should fit those needs like a well-tailored set of rails.

Step 1: Find the current stage

Take a moment to observe how the team interacts. In forming, people are polite, opinions are cautious, and roles are still being defined. In storming, disagreements rise, ownership lines blur, and friction can feel personal. In norming, members settle on ways of working, trust grows, and collaboration improves. In performing, the team runs smoothly, they solve problems together, and they optimize their workflow without heavy direction from you.

Step 2: Name the stage with the team

Face the reality: “We’re in forming,” or “We’re in storming.” Naming the stage creates a shared lens. It’s not labeling people; it’s clarifying the current dynamics so you can tailor actions precisely.

Step 3: Design stage-appropriate coaching actions

- Forming: clarify purpose, roles, and goals. Establish routines that foster early wins. Be explicit about expectations and how the team will communicate.

- Storming: create norms for healthy conflict, set ground rules for feedback, and facilitate structured discussions to surface concerns without blame. Your job is to steady the ship and keep focus on shared outcomes.

- Norming: reinforce collaboration, codify the best practices that emerged, and deepen trust. Start shifting more decision-making to the team and reduce your direct guidance as capacity grows.

- Performing: empower the team to set its own goals, optimize flow, and mentor newer members. Step back and let the team demonstrate autonomous problem-solving.

Step 4: Implement quick wins and visible progress

Choose small, observable actions that move the team forward within a few days. Quick wins might be clarifying a backlog item's acceptance criteria, refining a shared Definition of Ready, or establishing a regular rhythm for cross-functional reviews. When people see improvement early, confidence builds and momentum accelerates.

Step 5: Monitor signals and pivot as needed

Watch for telltale signs: communication clarity, backlog health, the rate at which decisions get made, and how quickly blockers are removed. If signals point to a different stage than you expected, adjust your coaching plan—don't double down on methods that aren't addressing the real need.

Examples and micro-cases

Case A: A brand-new team with five members from marketing, development, and QA. In the forming stage, meetings are quiet, action items pile up, and ownership is unclear. You introduce a simple set of roles (product owner, facilitator, technical lead, quality champion) and a 20-minute daily stand-up with clear questions: What did you do yesterday? What will you do today? What blockers stand in your way? Within two sprints, the team begins to volunteer for responsibilities, backlog items are clearly described, and interruptions drop as people start coordinating more smoothly.

Case B: A team that has been together for three months hits the storming stage. You run a structured retrospective focused on process rather than people, invite a rotating facilitator, and create a safety agreement that says "If it's hard to hear, we will pause and reframe." You also implement a lightweight conflict-resolution pact: disagreements are aired, but decisions are documented and revisited if outcomes aren't working. By sprint five, the team negotiates who owns which parts of the feature with less tension, and collaboration improves as trust grows.

Case C: A mature team enters norming and then performing. You begin reducing direct coaching while increasing peer coaching and cross-training. You help them map critical skills and rotate responsibilities so more members can cover for one another. The team cuts handoffs, shortens review cycles, and delivers value more consistently. They begin mentoring newer teams, sharing best practices, and aligning on a shared long-term plan.

Fostering Psychological Safety and Trust to Enable Risk-Taking

Psychological safety is the feeling that you can speak up, share ideas, and admit mistakes without fear of embarrassment or punishment. It matters because learning and improvement happen fastest when people can take informed risks and learn from what fails as well as what succeeds.

Step 1: Define safety as a team value

Have a brief, explicit conversation about why safety matters. Your goal is a clear, common understanding: people can voice concerns, ask questions, and propose experiments without ridicule or blame.

Step 2: Create predictable, respectful routines

Establish norms that protect dialogue. Round-robin speaking ensures everyone has a chance to contribute. A “no interruption” rule keeps ideas intact. A "pause and reframe" move helps when emotions rise.

Step 3: Normalize constructive feedback

Teach a simple feedback pattern: describe the behavior, explain the impact, and propose a concrete change. Emphasize that feedback is about improving outcomes, not judging people.

Step 4: Practice safe retrospectives

Frame retrospectives as experiments in learning. Encourage quiet participants to share first, celebrate small wins, and analyze failures as data rather than personal flaws.

Step 5: Respond calmly to risk-taking

When a team member suggests something risky, acknowledge the idea, ask clarifying questions, and discuss potential risks together. Your calm, curious stance invites more voices into the conversation.

Step 6: Measure warmth and trust

Use quick pulse checks or short surveys to gauge how safe people feel in meetings and planning sessions. Look for trends over time rather than one-off opinions. Adjust practices if trust isn't improving.

Examples and micro-cases

Case D: In a stand-up, a junior tester hints at a fragile area in a release plan. Instead of brushing it off, you invite the tester to walk the team through the concern and propose a small test. The team experiments with a brief risk assessment, and the plan is adjusted. The junior team member feels seen, and others start voicing concerns earlier in the cycle.

Case E: During a retrospective, a developer shares a failure they caused that delayed a feature. Instead of blaming, the team codes a learning item: "We will add an automated check for this scenario." The shared learning reduces similar issues in the next sprint and builds collective accountability.

Encouraging Cross-Functionality and Collective Ownership

Cross-functionality means team members bring a range of skills to work together rather than sticking to narrow roles. Collective ownership means the team as a whole is responsible for delivering value, not just individuals or subgroups.

Step 1: Map skills and responsibilities

Create a simple map of who can contribute to which parts of the work. This helps identify gaps and opportunities for cross-training. It also highlights potential bottlenecks caused by single points of failure.

Step 2: Create cross-functional ways of working

Form small, stable groups that include the necessary disciplines to complete end-to-end work. Establish shared goals and a combined backlog so the team can pull items together rather than passing them along the line.

Step 3: Align goals and measures

Agree on a single outcome the team is responsible for delivering in a short time frame. Tie success to observable results, such as faster delivery, higher quality, or improved user satisfaction.

Step 4: Reduce handoffs and handover friction

Track where handoffs slow things down and remove unnecessary steps. Where possible, co-locate or synchronize work calendars so team members can collaborate in real time.

Step 5: Practice rotating responsibilities

Let team members rotate through different roles on a regular basis—lead reviewer, tester, integration lead—so skills spread and understanding grows. This reduces bottlenecks and builds empathy.

Step 6: Create a shared ownership charter

Publish a short document that everyone signs, stating that the team owns the end-to-end outcome and that everyone is accountable for its success. This charter becomes a living guide for decisions and trade-offs.

Step 7: Normalize joint decision-making

When a decision affects multiple disciplines, require input from representatives of each area. Decisions are more durable when they reflect diverse expertise and perspectives.

Step 8: Celebrate joint wins

Highlight outcomes that only happened because the team collaborated, not because a single person solved the problem. Public recognition reinforces the value of cross-functional effort.

Step 9: Invest in cross-training

Offer lightweight learning sessions or shadowing opportunities so teammates understand each other's work. Cross-training pays off in smoother collaboration and faster problem solving.

Step 10: Build a sense of shared ownership

Create rituals that reinforce ownership, like a quarterly review of outcomes where the whole team analyzes what worked, what didn't, and what to try next.

Case studies and micro-cases

Case F: A product team formed a cross-functional "delivery pod" including developers, testers, UX, and a data analyst. They set a shared objective: reduce release cycle time by 20%. By working end-to-end on a single feature and rotating roles, the pod delivered a valuable update in half the usual time. The outcome: fewer bottlenecks, clearer accountability, and a stronger sense of teamwork.

Case G: A team struggling with last-minute surprises reorganized into stable cross-functional squads. They created a joint backlog and a weekly integration check-in where each member spoke to how their work affected others. The changes shaved hours off integration time and boosted morale as everyone felt responsible for the final product.

Exercises

1) Stage Map Sprint (15–20 minutes)

- Do this with the whole team. Draw a simple four-column map for Forming, Storming, Norming, Performing. Have each person place a sticky on the column that best fits the team's current behavior and a short note about what's needed to move to the next column. Expected outcome: a quick, visible diagnosis and a plan for the next few days.

2) Safety Norms Workshop (45 minutes)

- Agree on 5 core norms that protect psychological safety (for example, “no interruptions,” “assume positive intent,” “everyone speaks once in each meeting”). Write them on a shared board and capture examples of how you’ll apply them in a real meeting. Expected outcome: a concrete, agreed-upon safety framework.

3) Cross-Functional Pairing Plan (60 minutes)

- Pair up members from different disciplines and map one feature they could own together end-to-end. Define roles, boundaries, and a quick check-in rhythm. Expected outcome: a practical pair plan that reduces handoffs and increases mutual understanding.

4) Ownership Charter Crafting (30 minutes)

- Create a one-page charter that states the team's shared outcome, key responsibilities, and how success will be measured. Have each member sign it. Expected outcome: a tangible commitment to collective ownership.

Troubleshooting: Quick fixes for common problems

- Problem: The team stalls at Forming or slides into Storming again.

Quick fix: Reintroduce a short, low-stakes ritual that builds clarity and safety. Reconfirm roles, goals, and norms. Bring in a simple retrospective format that concentrates on process rather than people.

- Problem: Psychological safety is present only in some meetings, not all.

Quick fix: Normalize honest dialogue with a structured, blame-free feedback loop. Use round-robin sharing and silent brainstorming to give quieter voices a chance to be heard. If needed, split into smaller groups for sensitive topics and then reconvene.

- Problem: Cross-functional ownership feels shallow or temporary.

Quick fix: Tie the charter to real incentives and visible outcomes. Create a rotating responsibility schedule and a short monthly review that highlights joint success stories and concrete improvements to the workflow.

Tools and templates

- Team Stage Assessment (one-page)

Section headers: Team name, Members, Current Stage, Signs You See, Next Target Stage, Actions to Take.

- Safety Norms Checklist (one-page)

Five norms with simple examples of how to practice them in daily work.

- Cross-Functional Ownership Charter (one-page)

Outcome statement, Roles and Responsibilities, Shared Metrics, Review Cycle.

- Joint Outcomes Charter Template (one-page)

Objective, Timeframe, Metrics, Review Cadence, Sign-off.

Key Takeaway

Safety and shared ownership aren't add-ons; they are the gears that let a team learn, adapt, and perform together.

Coming up next

Coming up next: Subtittle: Facilitating Agile Ceremonies Effectively

1) Designing productive sprint planning and review sessions,

2) Running focused daily stand-ups and outcome-driven retrospectives,

3) Timeboxing, agenda-setting, and techniques for remote facilitation.

Chapter 4

Facilitating Agile Ceremonies Effectively

By the end of this chapter, you will be able to run sprint planning and review sessions that are clear, focused, and outcome-driven, while keeping daily stand-ups brief and retrospectives productive, even when you're facilitating remotely.

1) Designing productive sprint planning and review sessions

Prepare, aim, execute. The first step in any great planning session is to prepare the ground so the team can move fast when the clock starts. Before you gather everyone, make sure the backlog is in decent shape: items are described at a level that lets people discuss them, dependencies are noted, and any questions asking for clarity are visible. The goal you set for the sprint should be specific enough to guide the team but flexible enough to adapt if needed. A crisp sprint goal helps the group stay aligned even when new information appears.

Step 1: Prepare the backlog and define the sprint goal. Look over the items that could be addressed in the next sprint. Pick items that clearly support a small, achievable goal. If any item is fuzzy or risky, flag it for quick discussion rather than letting it stall planning. The reason you do this is simple: clarity at the start saves time during the meeting and reduces back-and-forth later. A well-scoped sprint goal acts like a compass, guiding the whole session.

Step 2: Select items to commit to and clarify done criteria. In the planning room, discuss which items will realistically fit the sprint. Make sure the team agrees on what "done" means for each item. A clear definition of done helps everyone know when to stop and ensures you have a reliable measure of progress. If acceptance tests or verification steps exist, name them together so there's no guessing after work starts.

Step 3: Create the plan and align with teammates. Turn the chosen items into a plan for the sprint. Decide who will work on what, and sketch a rough timeline that fits the team's capacity. If there are dependencies, map them out and decide who will address them first. The aim is not to lock everyone into one exact path but to have a shared plan that can adapt while still delivering a real result.

Step 4: Close with a compact plan and next actions. End the session with a short recap: the sprint goal, the items you will tackle, and who is responsible for which piece. Capture any follow-up questions and add them to the backlog. Close with a clear sense of momentum—everyone should leave knowing what comes next and what to watch for during the sprint.

Two quick micro-cases show how this works in real teams. In the first case, a small software team faced a sprint goal to improve a login flow. They prepared the backlog, defined what "done" looked like (including a demo to the product owner and passing basic tests), and agreed on who would work on the main stories. The result? The team started the sprint with a shared understanding, fewer mid-sprint questions, and a smoother demo at the end. In the second case, another team found ambiguity in several items. They spent extra time sharpening three items into small, testable tasks and added a simple acceptance note to each. The sprint ran more smoothly, and the product owner felt confident about what would be delivered.

2) Running focused daily stand-ups and outcome-driven retrospectives

Daily stand-ups and retrospectives are the heartbeat of agile work. Stand-ups keep the team synchronized and help blockers surface early.

Retrospectives turn experience into action, focusing on what to try next to improve outcomes.

Step 1: Structure the daily stand-up for outcomes. In a standing meeting, each person answers three simple questions: what they did yesterday, what they will do today, and what blocks their progress. The emphasis is not on a log of tasks but on the team's ability to move the work forward. To keep it tight, limit the meeting to a short timebox, and encourage people to share only what's necessary for others to proceed.

Step 2: Keep it timeboxed and visible. A common target is a 15-minute window. Use a shared board or wall where everyone can see the current work and blockers. A visible board helps people orient their updates without lengthy explanations. If a blocker stops progress, note it and assign ownership to remove it—do not let it linger in the air.

Step 3: Run outcome-driven retrospectives. After every sprint, gather the team to reflect on outcomes, not just tasks. A simple and effective format is to discuss what went well, what could be improved, and what the team will try next. The key is to pick one or two experiments that can reasonably be tested in the next sprint. Assign a owner and a deadline for checking the result. This approach keeps learning concrete and actionable.

Step 4: Document and follow up. Capture the chosen experiments, the owners, and the expected impact. At the start of the next sprint, review how those experiments played out and decide whether to scale them, tweak them, or retire them. The practice of planning, acting, and reflecting builds a steady rhythm the team can trust.

Two micro-cases illustrate the rhythm. In one team, daily stand-ups revealed a recurring blocker that slowed a front-end task. The team assigned a specific person to follow up on the blocker, changed a dependency order, and the work moved forward. In another team, the retrospective produced a small but powerful experiment: pair programming for high-traffic tasks. The outcome was a smoother onboarding experience for new members and a noticeable bump in delivery consistency.

3) Timeboxing, agenda-setting, and techniques for remote facilitation

Timeboxing is the discipline that keeps meetings efficient. Agenda-setting ensures everyone knows why you are meeting, what will happen, and how long it will take. Remote facilitation adds a layer of accessibility and inclusivity, since team members may be scattered across time zones and devices.

Step 1: Timebox the meeting and its parts. Decide the total length of the session first, then break it into equal, labeled chunks (for example, 15 minutes for setup, 30 minutes for discussion, 10 minutes for decisions). Announce these timeboxes at the start, and use a timer to stay honest. Timeboxing creates urgency and helps people focus on what matters most.

Step 2: Create a crisp agenda in advance. The agenda should list the purpose of the meeting, the topics to cover, who leads each topic, and the time allotted. Share it with the team ahead of time so people can prepare. A clear agenda reduces off-track conversations and makes the meeting easier to follow, even for new teammates.

Step 3: Define roles and rotate them. Assign a facilitator, a note-taker, and a timekeeper. If possible, rotate these roles so everyone practices facilitation skills and no single person bears all the work. The facilitator guides the flow, the note-taker captures decisions and follow-ups, and the timekeeper enforces the clock.

Step 4: Use remote facilitation techniques that fit distributed teams. In virtual rooms, position cameras so faces are visible, encourage turn-taking, and invite input from quieter voices. Use a shared digital board for real-time updates, and consider quick polls or short breakout discussions to gather input from different perspectives. For retrospectives, a simple technique is to collect inputs on color-coded cards (green for good, yellow for okay, red for challenges) and then group them to identify common themes.

Step 5: Address common remote challenges with quick fixes. When someone is quiet or connectivity falters, invite them to share in writing or assign a short check-in to bring them into the conversation. If the agenda runs long, pause, recap, and decide which items can be continued asynchronously or in a follow-up session. Remote meetings work best when participation is explicit and everyone knows their role in the flow.

Two micro-cases demonstrate remote facilitation success. In one example, a global team ran sprint planning using a shared online board and strict timeboxing. The process kept discussions efficient and produced a clear plan that all time zones could support. In another example, a distributed team ran a retrospective with a round-robin format, allowing each member to speak in turn. The outcome was a higher level of psychological safety and a set of practical experiments that were ready to try in the next sprint.

Key Takeaway: Clear, timebound ceremonies with a visible plan and shared ownership reduce confusion, speed up work, and create reliable momentum.

Coming up next Subtittle: Coaching Techniques and Powerful Conversations

1) Using probing questions, active listening, and structured feedback ,

2) Setting experiments and outcome-based goals with teams,

3) Adopting directive, collaborative, and inquiry-based coaching stances

Chapter 5

Coaching Techniques and Powerful Conversations

By the end of this chapter you will use probing questions, active listening, and structured feedback to guide teams toward clear experiments and constructive conversations.

Using probing questions, active listening, and structured feedback

1. Prepare probing questions that surface assumptions, goals, and constraints.

What you want to uncover is not just what happened, but why it happened and what people think about it. Start with open prompts that invite reflection rather than defense. Ask questions that reveal assumptions, priorities, and early warning signs. For example: What outcome are we hoping to achieve with this sprint? What would make this plan fail, in your view? If we keep doing what we're doing, what's the most likely result in two weeks? Write a short list of 6–8 prompts you can pull from in conversations, and adapt them as you hear answers. The goal is to move from surface details to deeper patterns without pushing people into a fight or a defensive stance. A good question creates clarity; a great question creates momentum.

2. Practice active listening: listen to understand, not to respond.

Active listening means more than hearing words. It means noticing tone, pause, and emotion; then reflecting back what you heard so the speaker feels seen and understood. Use a simple cycle: paraphrase what was said, summarize the core point, and note the impact you heard. For instance: "So you're saying the backlog feels crowded because we're trying to fit too many stories into one sprint, which makes planning feel rushed." Then check for accuracy: "Did I get that right?" If you miss something, gently correct yourself and keep listening. When you reflect feelings as well as content, you create psychological safety and make people willing to share honest observations rather than guard themselves. A practical habit is to pause after a speaker finishes, give a quiet moment, and then respond with what you heard rather than immediately offering your own ideas.

3. Use structured feedback to keep conversations productive.

Structured feedback helps everyone understand what happened, what it did to others, and what to do next. A common and simple model is Situation-Behavior-Impact. Describe the situation, state the observable behavior, and explain the impact on the team or goal. Then offer a concrete suggestion for next steps. For example: "In yesterday's stand-up (Situation), you interrupted twice (Behavior), which slowed the team from confirming the next steps (Impact). Next time, can we let each person finish before others respond, so we capture all perspectives before deciding?" Keep feedback timely, specific, and focused on observable actions rather than personal traits. If you notice tension rising, acknowledge it briefly and steer back to concrete behavior and outcomes. A practical tip is to separate feedback from praise and critique so both land clearly: praise for what went well, and precise guidance for what to adjust.

4. Practice a focused conversation using the three tools together.

In a real session, combine probing questions, active listening, and structured feedback in a tight loop. Start with a probing question to set the direction. Listen actively to the answer and reflect it back to confirm understanding. Then give structured feedback on what you observed and suggest the next concrete step. Repeat only as needed to reach a clear, actionable agreement. For example, in a sprint retrospective, you might ask: “What’s one assumption we’re making about our workflow?” Listen, reflect, and then say: “The impact of that assumption is slowing us down because we plan for more tasks than we can complete. Let’s test a small change in the next sprint: limit our planning to a fixed number of high-priority stories.” This isn’t about delivering orders; it's about guiding understanding and agreement through a disciplined dialogue.

Micro-cases to illustrate the three tools in action

Micro-case A: A team misses a sprint goal because of unclear priorities. You ask, "What outcome are we aiming for with this sprint? How does each item contribute to that outcome?" You listen, paraphrase: "So the team feels the backlog is crowded and items are competing for attention." You offer structured feedback: "Let's test a stricter backlog refinement by focusing on the top three priorities and delaying others until we're done." Outcome: the team aligns on priorities and reduces last-minute changes.

Micro-case B: During a daily stand-up, a developer sounds frustrated about blockers. You probe gently: "What would a successful day look like for you right now?" Listen for specifics and reflect: "You need a decision on a dependency before you can proceed." Then you give feedback with a next step: "We'll route that dependency decision to the right owner by EOD, and in the meantime you'll focus on the tasks you can do without that blocker." Outcome: clarity increases, blockers get routed, and momentum returns.

Micro-case C: In a mid-project review, a team member feels the team isn't hearing their point about a risk. You ask, "What would make this risk clearer to everyone?" You listen, acknowledge the concern, and respond with structured feedback: "Your point is that the risk could slow delivery by two days. Let's document the risk with specific probability and impact, and decide whether to add a mitigation action." Outcome: risk is documented and mitigations are planned, not postponed.

Common pitfalls and quick fixes

- Pitfall: Asking one big question and stopping. Fix: Break complex questions into smaller steps and allow space for responses.

- Pitfall: Listening to reply instead of listening to understand. Fix: After someone speaks, summarize their point before adding your own ideas.

- Pitfall: Giving too much advice at once. Fix: Offer one concrete action per conversation and ask for agreement before proceeding.

- Pitfall: Judging or debating. Fix: Keep feedback about behavior and outcomes; avoid labeling people.

Setting experiments and outcome-based goals with teams

1. Define a focused experiment with a clear hypothesis.

An experiment is a small, time-limited test designed to learn something new. Start with a question you want to answer, such as: “If we shorten daily stand-ups to 10 minutes and focus on blockers, will we finish stories faster this week?” Turn that into a simple hypothesis: “If we shorten the stand-up to a fixed time and strictly address blockers, we will complete one more story per sprint.” Write it down in plain language, and keep it to a single, testable idea. The goal is to learn, not prove a point. A well-phrased hypothesis helps you measure success and decide quickly whether to adopt, adjust, or discard the change.

2. Set outcome-based goals with clear success criteria.

An outcome-based goal describes what you want to achieve, not just what you will do. Instead of "improve planning," say, "increase sprint goal completion to 90% by the end of three sprints." Define how you will measure success, the time frame, and what signals will show progress. Think in observable effects: more predictable delivery, fewer last-minute changes, clearer ownership of tasks. Make the goal visible to the team, and agree on what data will count as evidence. Timeboxing your experiment helps you learn quickly and avoid dragging out tests that don't yield signal.

3. Plan the experiment with steps and responsibilities.

Draft a simple plan: what you will change, who will try it, what data you will collect, and when you will review results. Keep the plan lightweight so it doesn't require a separate project to track. For example, if you want to test a new daily stand-up format, decide who will lead, what the new format looks like, how you'll measure impact, and when you'll evaluate. Decide how you will record results—an easy checklist, a short note in the retro, or a one-page summary. The aim is to make the test easy to run and easy to stop if it doesn't help.

4. Run the experiment and collect data with minimal overhead.

Use simple, quick methods to gather evidence: counting completed stories, tracking blockers resolved, or collecting a quick sentiment note at the end of the day. Don't drown the team in data. The best signals are few but clear. Keep the observation process light and consistent so you can compare results across cycles. If the data doesn't show a clear trend, be ready to pivot or stop the experiment. The point is learning, not proving.

5. Review results and decide next steps.

After the test period, gather the data and discuss what happened. Ask: Did the outcome move as expected? What surprised us? What would we do next? Map the results to your hypothesis and decide whether to adopt the change, tweak it, or drop it. Frame the decision as a new knowledge item: "We learned that shortening stand-ups improved focus on blockers but reduced quick status updates; we'll try a hybrid format next sprint." Clear reflection is the bridge from experiment to continuous improvement.

Micro-cases to illustrate experiments in action

Micro-case D: A team wants to improve alignment on priorities. You propose a small experiment: "For the next two sprints, we will run a lighter planning session that concentrates on the top three backlog items only." Hypothesis: this will speed up planning and improve focus. Outcome: planning time decreases and sprint goals become smoother. Decision: adopt the three-item focus with minor tweaks.

Micro-case E: A team struggles with blockers that stall progress. You set an experiment to document blockers in a shared board and assign owners for blocking issues. Hypothesis: making blockers visible and assigning owners will reduce waiting time. Outcome: blockers are resolved more quickly, and delivery becomes steadier. Decision: keep the new blocking process and refine the ownership flow.

Common pitfalls and quick fixes for experiments

- Pitfall: Too big a change for a short test. Fix: pick a single variable and keep the experiment small.

- Pitfall: Vague success criteria. Fix: define clear, observable outcomes and a concrete deadline.

- Pitfall: Data collection gets out of hand. Fix: use one or two simple metrics that directly reflect the outcome.

- Pitfall: Skipping a formal review. Fix: schedule a short retro to discuss what the data says and what to do next.

Adopting directive, collaborative, and inquiry-based coaching stances

1. Define the three stances clearly and know when to use each.

Directive coaching gives clear guidance and decisions when timing matters or when teams lack direction. Collaborative coaching invites the team to participate in decisions, fostering ownership. Inquiry-based coaching uses questions to spark discovery and self-generated solutions. Each stance has a purpose, and you switch between them as needed. The best coaches don't stay in one stance; they read the room and switch to the most effective approach in the moment.

2. Recognize cues that signal the right stance to use.

If a team looks stuck and needs a concrete plan, a directive approach can help move things forward. If the team feels capable but wants to own the path, collaboration works well. If people are held back by assumptions or blind spots, an inquiry approach can unlock new thinking. Quick signs include: levels of confusion, ownership of outcomes, and willingness to propose ideas. Your job is to match the method to the moment, not to force one style on every situation.

3. Move between stances intentionally during a session.

Start with curiosity and questions to surface issues (inquiry). If you hear repeated dead ends, offer a pragmatic framework or a decision to move forward (directive). When the team shows energy and capability, shift toward co-creating options together (collaborative). A practical pattern is to begin with questions, transition to a concise plan or decision, and then invite the team to refine the plan in a collaborative way. In a coaching chat with a team lead, you might ask: "What outcomes do you own, and what decisions would you like me to make for you?" Then, after listening, you propose a concrete step and invite team input.

4. Use stances to protect safety while driving progress.

Inquiry-based coaching often builds psychological safety because it centers on listening and discovery. Directive coaching can accelerate results, but used too often it can suppress voice. Collaborative coaching balances both by asking for input and accelerating momentum through shared decisions. When you mix stances wisely, you help teams grow confidence while still delivering outcomes.

5. Common pitfalls and quick fixes for coaching stances

- Pitfall: Always forcing a directive stance. Fix: Pause and ask a question to surface alternatives before directing.

- Pitfall: Only using inquiry and never making progress. Fix: When the team stalls, offer a concise plan or decision to regain movement.

- Pitfall: Taking ownership away from the team. Fix: Frame guidance as a support to the team's own decision-making rather than a takeover.

Key Takeaway: The right questions, careful listening, and clear feedback shield the coaching conversation from confusion and build real progress.

Coming up next Subtittle: Metrics, Measurement, and Driving Improvement

1) Selecting meaningful metrics beyond velocity and vanity stats,

2) Interpreting data to form hypotheses and guide experiments,

3) Embedding feedback loops into regular workflows and retrospectives

Chapter 6

Metrics, Measurement, and Driving Improvement

You will gain the ability to pick metrics that reflect real progress, turn data into testable ideas, and weave feedback loops into daily work to drive real improvement.

1. Selecting meaningful metrics beyond velocity and vanity stats

Metrics should illuminate value, flow, and quality, not just the number of tasks completed. Velocity is a familiar number, but it often hides the true health of a team's process. When you choose metrics, start with what the team actually wants to change, not what the team has always measured. The goal is to see work flow, bottlenecks, and learning in a way that invites action, not guilt or bragging.

Define outcomes first. If your aim is faster delivery of customer value, your metrics should reveal how quickly value moves from idea to usable product. If your aim is higher quality, you'll want metrics that reveal defect rates, rework, and how often work items slip back into earlier stages. If your aim is more reliable planning, you'll look at predictability and stability across sprints. Avoid metrics that are easy to measure but don't tell you whether you're moving toward your goal.

Pick 3–5 core metrics and lean on them. Too many metrics scatter attention and create confusion. Choose a small, coherent set that covers flow, quality, and reliability. For example, you might select lead time, cycle time, throughput, defect rate, and a measure of customer value delivered. Lead time tracks the span from work starting to completion, giving you a sense of how fast you can deliver. Cycle time, from when work actually begins to completion, helps you spot delays within the production process. Throughput tells you how many items you complete in a period, giving you a sense of cadence. Defect rate or escape rate shows how often issues escape into production and require rework. Customer value delivered ties the team's work to real outcomes, if you have a way to quantify value.

Make data collectible and actionable. Metrics should be things you can observe, influence, and improve. If you can affect WIP limits, you should be able to see how those limits change lead time or throughput. If you can adjust testing or review times, you should be able to observe changes in defect rates. Keep dashboards simple, and ensure every metric has a clear question it answers. For instance: “What is our average lead time this sprint, and did it improve after adjusting WIP limits?” or “Did the defect rate drop after we added automated tests in the sprint?”

Concrete micro-case. Suppose your team tracks lead time and discovers that, during the last three sprints, average lead time crept from about 3 days to 7 days. That’s a red flag: something in the flow is slowing us down. You test a hypothesis by introducing a modest WIP limit and clarifying the definition of “done” for each item. After a couple of sprints, you see lead time fall back to around 4 days, and you also notice fewer items are blocked by wait times in testing. The numbers move in the direction you want, and you can point to a concrete change that helped.

Another micro-case. A team spots a rising defect escape rate after increasing the sprint scope. They pause new feature work for one sprint, review the root causes in the retro, and implement a stricter "definition of ready" and more automated checks. The defect rate drops, and the team returns to steady velocity with fewer disruptions in production. These stories show how metrics are not just numbers; they're signals you can act on.

Watch for vanity metrics. A number that sounds impressive but doesn't connect to real outcomes can mislead. For example, “stories completed” each sprint might rise while customer value remains flat, or lead time stays long because work is piling up in queues. Your job is to translate the signal into a meaningful action. If a metric doesn’t inform a decision, prune it from the dashboard. Keep the focus on what moves the needle for your goals.

Pitfalls and quick fixes. A common trap is chasing metrics for bragging rights rather than learning. If people start gaming numbers, you’ll lose trust and skew the data. To avoid this, keep metrics honest by making data visible to the whole team, inviting questions, and tying metrics to concrete experiments. If data looks inconsistent, don’t panic—investigate and corroborate with multiple indicators. Use smaller, repeatable tests to confirm what you're seeing before you make big changes.

Two quick examples to illustrate the point. First, a team notices velocity climbs while lead time lengthens. They interpret this as a problem, not success, because customers feel the lengthier wait. They introduce tighter WIP limits and add a quicker review process. Lead time improves, and velocity stabilizes at a healthier level. Second, a team tracks customer value delivered and discovers that several small features aren't moving value meaningfully. They reprioritize to a few high-value items and shorten the feedback loop with customers, which lifts satisfaction without expanding the sprint backlog.

2. Interpreting data to form hypotheses and guide experiments

Data becomes useful when you turn it into questions you can test. The goal is to convert a trend into a small, testable hypothesis and then run a controlled, time-limited experiment. This keeps learning moving and reduces the risk of big, unfounded changes.

Look for patterns across multiple data points. A single spike in a metric is interesting but not enough to draw conclusions. Look for repeated movements, clusters, or consistent relationships between metrics. For example, you might notice that when WIP increases above a certain threshold, lead time tends to grow and defect rate tends to rise as well. That pattern becomes a hypothesis: "If we cap WIP at X items, lead time and defect rate will improve."

Form a testable hypothesis. Phrase it as a simple, testable statement you can confirm or refute in a short time. For instance: "Reducing WIP by 25% for two sprints will lower average lead time by 15% without reducing throughput." Keep the hypothesis concrete, measurable, and within your control. If you can't influence it directly, reframe the question to something you can change with a safe experiment.

Design small, time-bound experiments. Short cycles keep risk low and learning high. Choose a duration that fits your sprint rhythm—often one to two sprints. Define the experiment's conditions, the metrics you'll monitor, and what will count as a successful outcome. Then run the experiment, collect data, and review it with the team in a retrospective or a dedicated data review session.

Make space for learning. Treat every experiment as a step in a larger learning loop. Some experiments will confirm your hypothesis, others will refute it, and some will yield unexpected insights. Either result is valuable as long as you capture what you learned and adjust your approach accordingly. Document the insight, not just the result, so you can repeat the learning process in future work.

Two micro-cases to show the thinking in action. Case A: A team notices that cycle time rose when stories required heavy manual testing. They hypothesize that automated testing will speed delivery. They implement a small batch of automated tests in one area of the product for two sprints and measure cycle time, defect rate, and throughput. The data shows a modest drop in cycle time and a reduction in defects in that area, confirming the value of the automation effort and guiding broader rollout. Case B: A team observes that customer-reported issues spike after new features ship. Their hypothesis is simple: "Increasing early customer feedback will reduce post-release issues." They run a one-sprint experiment by inviting customers to test early builds and give feedback through a lightweight beta program. The feedback loop shortens, issues surface earlier, and the team reduces last-minute rework, reinforcing the habit of early validation.

Be practical with data interpretation. Always connect your interpretation to an action. If a trend exists, translate it into a small change that you can test in the next sprint. If the trend is unclear, refine your measurement or add a second metric to clarify the signal. The aim is not to collect more data, but to gain clearer, faster, more actionable insights that lead to better decisions and better results.

3. Embedding feedback loops into regular workflows and retrospectives

Feedback loops are the heartbeat of adaptive teams. They keep learning aligned with action and help teams adjust quickly in the face of change. The trick is to weave feedback into the daily rhythm, not to bolt it on as an extra duty.

Make metrics review a regular ceremony. Add a lightweight review of the key metrics into your sprint planning or your weekly team stand-up. A simple question like, “What does the data say this week, and what will we test next sprint to improve it?” keeps attention on evidence rather than emotion. The goal is a two-way conversation: the data informs decisions, and the team’s hypotheses guide what to improve next.

Incorporate experiments into retrospectives. Use retros as a place to turn data into action. When you finish a sprint, review the metrics for the sprint and identify one small experiment to run in the next sprint. Frame it as a concrete action: "We will reduce WIP to improve lead time." Assign ownership, set a time box, and decide how you'll measure success. The best experiments are small, reversible, and tied to a clear outcome.

Create a visible, accessible feedback loop. Build a simple dashboard or a one-page scorecard that lives in a common space where everyone can see it. Make it easy to interpret: one line for lead time, one for cycle time, one for throughput, one for defect rate, one for customer value. The team should be able to understand the direction of travel at a glance and ask questions without needing a data specialist. When dashboards are accessible, feedback becomes a natural habit rather than a separate task.

Embed regular reflection with stakeholders. Periodically invite product owners, customers, or other stakeholders into the data review to align on outcomes. Share what the data is saying and invite input on interpretation and experiments. This helps ensure transparency and keeps everyone moving toward the same outcomes, not into separate power plays or isolated improvements.

Two micro-cases to illustrate feedback loops in action. Case A: After a sprint, the team notices lead time improving but customer value delivered remains flat. In the retrospective, they test a hypothesis that value alignment is missing in refinement. They adjust the backlog grooming to include early customer value checks, track a simple value-delivery metric, and see value numbers rise in the next sprint while lead time remains healthy.

Case B: A distributed team uses a shared dashboard and a weekly data review. They identify a bottleneck in integration testing that appears during mid-sprint. They reallocate testing resources mid-sprint and establish a fast feedback channel with the QA team. In a few weeks, throughput stabilizes and defects drop, because feedback and adjustments happen quickly.

Exercises

1) Map your outcomes to metrics. Time: 20 minutes. What outcomes do you care about in your team's work? Write down 3–5 outcomes and map them to potential metrics. Check that every metric you pick is directly linked to at least one outcome. Measure progress by listing the metrics and the specific question each one answers.

2) Design a simple two-sprint data collection plan. Time: 30 minutes. Choose 2–3 metrics and decide how you will collect data for them over the next two sprints. Write down the data sources, who collects what, and how you will review the results at

the end of sprint 2. Check progress by confirming you can generate a chart or a quick snapshot for each metric.

3) Run a one-sprint experiment to test a change in flow. Time: 1 sprint. Pick one actionable change (for example, a modest WIP limit or a faster feedback loop in testing). Define the hypothesis, the metrics you'll watch, and the acceptance criteria for success. At sprint end, review whether the data supports the hypothesis and decide what to do next.

4) Build a lightweight dashboard and share it. Time: 45 minutes. Create a one-page dashboard with 4–5 core metrics. Make it readable at a glance.

Share it with the team and a stakeholder audience. Collect quick feedback on clarity and usefulness, then refine.

Troubleshooting notes

- If metrics drift without clear cause, pause to re-check data collection methods. A misread data source can produce false signals. Reconfirm what each metric measures and ensure data is captured consistently.

- If a metric becomes a pressure point rather than a guide, prune it from the dashboard. Metrics should empower learning, not create fear or competition.

- If experiments fail to produce learning, reframe the hypothesis or adjust the experiment's scope. Small, reversible experiments reduce risk and increase the chance of meaningful insight.

- If stakeholders push back on metrics, focus on shared outcomes and invite their questions. Use their perspective to refine what you measure and how you act on the data.

Tools and templates

- A simple metric map: Outcome -> Metric(s) -> What you'll observe -> How you'll act.

- A two-sprint data plan template: sprint window, data sources, responsible person, data collection method, review plan.

- A one-page dashboard template: metric name, current value, trend, interpretation, action.

Key Takeaway: Choose a small, coherent set of metrics that connect directly to real outcomes, monitor them consistently, and use the data to drive fast, testable improvements.

Coming up next: Engaging Stakeholders and Leading Change

1) Aligning leadership on desired outcomes and success measures,

2) Managing resistance, expectations, and political dynamics,

3) Crafting a change plan that sustains adoption and learning

Chapter 7

Engaging Stakeholders and Leading Change

By the end of this chapter, you will know how to align leaders around clear outcomes, manage resistance, and craft a change plan that keeps learning alive.

1. Aligning leadership on desired outcomes and success measures

When you start any large change in how a team works, the first obstacle is mixed signals. Different leaders see different wins. Some focus on speed; others on quality or safety; still others on cost. Your job is to get everyone pulling in the same direction with a shared sense of what success looks like. That means uncovering the true goals, choosing a small set of meaningful measures, and agreeing on how you'll know you're making progress.

Step 1: Convene a leadership alignment session and frame a joint aim.

What you do: Gather the key leaders who will sponsor or influence the change—product, engineering, operations, customer support, and any other critical voices. Start with a single, clear aim.

Do not overload it with too many ambitions. For example, you might say, “Our aim is to deliver value to customers faster by shortening our cycle from idea to feedback while maintaining quality and stability.” Have each leader contribute one concrete criterion that matters to them, then distill this into a shared one-page aim.

Why it matters: A single, well-communicated aim reduces drift. It creates a common language you can reference in every meeting, every backlog refinement, and every retrospective. It also helps you discern trade-offs when conflicts appear—if one department wants to push velocity at the expense of reliability, you can revisit the shared aim together.

Step 2: Define success measures that matter and are observable.

What you do: Pick 3–4 simple, observable metrics that reflect the shared aim. Examples include cycle time or lead time, defect rate or quality signals, customer satisfaction, and team engagement or retention. Write them in plain language so anyone can understand. Be explicit about what "better" looks like (faster, cheaper, safer, higher quality) and how you'll measure it (a dashboard, a weekly review, a simple scorecard).

Why it matters: Clear measures turn abstract goals into tangible progress. They also create a feedback loop so leaders can see whether changes are helping or hurting. Without shared metrics, you'll end up with competing narratives about what "success" means.

Step 3: Create a shared outcomes map and get sign-off.

What you do: Build a one-page outcomes map that links the aim to the 3–4 success measures, to the teams involved, to the kinds of changes you'll try (processes, ceremonies, roles, tooling), and to a simple review cadence. Have leaders review, discuss, and sign off. Leave room for adjustments—this map is a living document, not a contract carved in stone.

Why it matters: A signed map creates public accountability. It signals that leadership will back the changes you implement and gives you a reference point when you need to explain decisions or recalibrate.

Examples and micro-cases:

- Case A: A software group aimed to reduce cycle time while keeping bug counts steady. They gathered product, design, engineering, and QA leaders in one room, drafted an aim line, and settled on cycle time as the primary metric with quality as a guardrail. After agreeing, they published a public one-page map and reviewed it weekly. Within a quarter, cycle time dropped while customer-reported quality stayed steady, and leaders began citing the map in exec updates.

- Case B: A product team sought faster delivery but worried about operational overhead. They focused on a single, shared metric: time-to-feedback from customer use. They defined "customer feedback" clearly (surveys, usage analytics, direct user interviews) and tracked it alongside cycle time. The sign-off session helped all leaders see how reducing handoffs would require changes in ceremonies and roles, not just a new tool.

Rationales and practical notes:

- Keep the aim simple and measurable. Too many metrics cause confusion and disputing.

- Involve diverse voices early. Leaders from different areas can surface hidden dependencies and constraints that affect the plan.

- Treat the map as a living document. Revisit it at set intervals to reflect what you've learned and what's changed in the environment.

2. Managing resistance, expectations, and political dynamics

Even with a clear aim, people resist change. Resistance isn't automatic opposition; it's fear of losing control, fear of failure, or fear of extra workload. Your job is to recognize it, listen, and address it openly. You'll also encounter political dynamics—who benefits, who loses, who has influence. You can navigate this by mapping interests, setting transparent rules, and creating early, visible wins that demonstrate value.

Step 1: Identify resistance and map stakeholders.

What you do: Do a quick stakeholder scan. List who will be affected by the changes, who has influence, who is undecided, and who might oppose the shift. Create a simple map that shows interests, concerns, and what each stakeholder needs to see to support the change. Have direct conversations with anxious or skeptical voices. Listen first, then ask clarifying questions.

Why it matters: Understanding where resistance comes from helps you tailor communication and changes. You'll avoid surprises during reviews and can preempt friction with early, targeted engagement.

Step 2: Set transparent expectations and governance rules.

What you do: Define who makes which decisions and how information will flow. Establish cadence for updates, decisions, and conflict resolution. Publish a short governance charter that outlines roles, responsibilities, and escalation paths. Make it easy for people to see how decisions are made and who they can talk to if something feels unclear.

Why it matters: Clear governance reduces back-channel noise and political maneuvering. When people know how decisions are made, they're more willing to participate honestly and to test new ways of working without fear of punitive outcomes.

Step 3: Build early wins and visible evidence of progress.

What you do: Identify a small, contained area where you can demonstrate rapid benefits. This might be a single feature team adopting a new planning rhythm, a pilot initiative to streamline a recurring handoff, or a lightweight change to improve testing and feedback. Track and celebrate the improvement publicly—short demos, dashboards, or success stories shared in team meetings.

Why it matters: Early wins create momentum and credibility. They show that the change is practical and worthwhile, which helps quiet resistance and turns skeptics into supporters.

Examples and micro-cases:

- Case C: A global team faced resistance from multiple departments worried about extra meetings. They mapped stakeholders, clarified who owned decisions about ceremonies, and committed to a 60-day pilot with monthly reviews. The governance charter made escalation simple, and the pilot delivered a clear uptick in feedback speed.

Leadership began citing the pilot as evidence that the approach was feasible rather than theoretical.

- Case D: A care-focused organization was concerned that changing routines might slow down service delivery. They produced a small set of experiments with strict time boxes and defined what "success" would look like for each experiment. The experiments rolled out quickly, with teams showing measurable improvements in both speed and customer satisfaction, which helped to ease concerns across the leadership group.

Practical notes on resistance and politics:

- Don't try to eliminate all resistance. Some friction helps keep you honest and focused. The goal is to surface concerns early and address them, not to pretend everything is perfect from day one.

- Communicate in multiple channels. Some people respond to written updates; others prefer short video chats or in-person conversations. Use a mix to increase understanding and buy-in.

- Be fair and patient. Political dynamics shift when people feel respected and included. If you're neutral and transparent, you reduce the risk that decisions feel imposed.

3. Crafting a change plan that sustains adoption and learning

A change plan isn't a one-time document; it's a living blueprint for how you'll keep learning, adapting, and improving. The best plans lay out milestones, learning loops, and ways to keep the momentum going after the initial push. They connect to daily work and to the rhythms teams already follow, so the change becomes part of how things get done, not an extra burden.

Step 1: Build a flexible change plan with milestones and learning loops.

What you do: Draft a plan that includes a few clear milestones (e.g., three month, six month targets) and assigns owners for each milestone. Embed learning loops—after every major event (planning, release, retrospective), pause to capture what worked, what didn't, and what to adjust. Keep the plan adaptable so you can revise it as you learn.

Why it matters: A flexible plan respects reality and avoids rigid, brittle processes. It helps teams stay invested because they see that the plan evolves with experience, not against it.

Step 2: Align the plan with existing processes and rhythms.

What you do: Tie the change activities to the team's current cadences—daily stand-ups, sprint cycles, review meetings, and quarterly planning where appropriate. Where possible, piggyback on already scheduled events to minimize extra overhead. Make it easy for teams to integrate the change into what they already do, rather than adding new, isolated rituals.

Why it matters: Alignment reduces friction and makes adoption feel natural. When a change slots into familiar routines, teams are more likely to use it consistently and to sustain it over time.

Step 3: Establish ongoing coaching, feedback, and adaptation.

What you do: Create a steady groove of coaching and feedback. Schedule regular check-ins with team leads, create a lightweight coaching circle where leaders can share experiences, and set up simple feedback channels—surveys, quick interviews, or a shared log of lessons learned. Make it normal to adjust the plan based on what you learn and to celebrate improvements as they appear.

Why it matters: Change is a process, not a project. Ongoing coaching keeps motivation high, reinforces learning, and reduces the chance that a good practice slides back into old habits.

Examples and micro-cases:

- Case E: A mid-sized tech firm built a six-month change plan that tied to existing quarterly reviews. They added a short "lessons learned" segment at the end of every sprint review, which fed into the next change cycle. This structure helped teams see steady improvement and kept leadership informed about what was working and what needed adjustment.

- Case F: A public-service department linked the change plan to their annual improvement plan. They created a small internal community of practice that met monthly to discuss results, share templates, and align on next steps. The plan stayed alive because it was reinforced in a structured, recurring way rather than as a one-off initiative.

Troubleshooting: common problems and quick fixes

- Problem: Leaders sign off but don't follow through. Quick fix: schedule brief, recurring check-ins tied to milestones; publicly acknowledge and document small wins to maintain accountability.

- Problem: Resistance resurfaces after initial optimism. Quick fix: re-visit the stakeholder map, re-state the shared aim, and adjust the plan to address new concerns; invite skeptical voices to co-design the next cycle.

- Problem: Change feels like extra work. Quick fix: demonstrate how new practices save time or improve outcomes in concrete terms; reduce manual steps by integrating into existing workflows or tools.

- Problem: Metrics drift or become vanity signals. Quick fix: set a clear governance rule that every metric has a purpose linked to the aim; remove or replace metrics that don't drive useful decisions.

Tools, templates, and quick-starts

- Stakeholder map template: a simple grid listing stakeholders, their concerns, expected benefits, and how you'll engage them.

- Change plan outline: milestones, owners, learning loops, and alignment with existing rhythms.

- Governance charter: roles, decision rights, escalation paths, and cadence for reviews.

- Outcome map one-pager: aim, success measures, teams involved, required changes, and review cadence.

- Early-win playbook: a small, time-boxed experiment with a defined scope, success criteria, and a plan to showcase the results.

Key Takeaway: Clear, early alignment on outcomes, open handling of resistance, and a flexible, learning-centered change plan are the best tools you have to keep agile adoption alive and growing.

Coming up next

Subtittle: Scaling Agile Across Teams and Programs

1) Coordinating dependencies and cross-team collaboration patterns,

2) Structures for scaling: feature teams, value streams, and communities,

3) Ensuring alignment, governance, and program-level flow

Chapter 8

Scaling Agile Across Teams and Programs

You will learn how to coordinate dependencies across teams and design scalable structures that keep multiple teams aligned and moving toward the same goals.

Coordinating dependencies and cross-team collaboration patterns

When many teams work together, no one team can own the entire outcome. Dependencies—where one team's work depends on another's—become the rhythm that can slow every delivery if not managed well. Your job is to create a predictable cadence and a shared language so teams can coordinate without shouting across walls.

Step 1: Map dependencies across teams. Start by listing the major streams of work that touch one another. One simple way is to draw a grid or map that shows which teams rely on which others for inputs, decisions, or timelines. Keep it visual and current. The goal is to see bottlenecks before they stall progress. Rationale: visibility reduces surprises and helps you plan around inevitable overlaps.

Step 2: Align planning cadences and release calendars. Establish regular planning intervals that synchronize across teams—these can be quarterly, monthly, or tied to major milestones. Create a lightweight program calendar that marks integration points, demo days, and decision gates. Rationale: alignment minimizes last-minute handoffs and creates structured moments for coordination.

Step 3: Create clear ownership for dependencies. Assign owners who are responsible for communicating status, negotiating trade-offs, and clearing blockers. These aren't solo roles; they're shared responsibilities across teams that require regular check-ins. Rationale: accountability speeds resolution and makes escalation unnecessary.

Step 4: Build simple integration rituals and environments. Establish a common cadence for testing, integration builds, and demo sessions where teams show progress toward shared milestones. Use a minimal set of integration environments and a clear "definition of done" for cross-team deliverables. Rationale: frequent, low-friction checks prevent misalignments from piling up.

Two micro-cases illustrate the approach in action. Case A involves a front-end team and a back-end API team. The API team publishes a stable contract every two weeks; the front-end team follows a synchronized sprint cycle and uses a shared integration build that automatically validates API changes. When a breaking change is detected, both teams pause and review the contract, then re-run tests together. This keeps the user-visible feature delivery on track without endless rework. Case B uses a mobile app team and a data services team. They share a quarterly milestone for a new data-driven feature and use a joint backlog that maps user stories to data service capabilities. The teams hold a monthly cross-team review to adjust timing, capacity, and priorities, ensuring that the feature lands with solid data integrity and a smooth user experience.

What tends to trip teams up here? Hidden dependencies, late decisions, and unclear ownership. Quick fixes include keeping the dependency map living (update it every sprint, not once a year), naming owners for all major dependencies, and instituting a short, focused cross-team review every two weeks. If a dependency shifts, you adjust the plan on the fly rather than pretending nothing changed. The better you get at spotting and addressing interdependencies, the less your progress will be derailed by someone else's delay.

Key takeaway: Visibility, synchronized planning, and clear ownership turn potential blockers into predictable checkpoints rather than roadblocks.

Structures for scaling: feature teams, value streams, and communities

To scale effectively, you need structures that can deliver value across multiple teams without creating chaos. Three common structures help teams coordinate at scale: feature teams, value streams, and communities of practice. Each has a role, a natural rhythm, and a simple covenant that keeps things moving without overwhelming teams with process overhead.

Step 1: Define feature teams that can own end-to-end slices of value. A feature team is a cross-functional unit capable of delivering a complete feature or customer-facing capability. They include designers, developers, testers, and sometimes data analysts, all focused on a shared outcome. Rationale: end-to-end ownership reduces handoffs and speeds feedback loops.

Step 2: Map value streams to show how work flows from idea to customer. A value stream is the end-to-end path that delivers value, from concept through development to delivery and support. It helps leaders see where investments produce the most impact and where handoffs cause bottlenecks.

Rationale: value streams provide a clearer connection between strategic goals and daily work, guiding where to align teams and resources.

Step 3: Establish communities of practice for knowledge sharing. Communities of practice are voluntary groups where people who share roles or interests (for example, testing, UX, accessibility, or data engineering) meet regularly to share learning, tools, and patterns. Rationale: shared learning accelerates improvement and keeps teams from reinventing the wheel.

Step 4: Create governance with lightweight decision rights. Define who decides what at the program level, who reviews and approves changes, and how teams escalate conflicts. Keep governance slim so it supports, not stifles, momentum. Rationale: clear governance reduces frictions and keeps teams moving toward shared outcomes.

Two micro-cases help you see these structures in action. Case 1 shows how feature teams operate in a mid-sized product. The organization splits into two feature teams—one focused on core functionality and one on extension features. Each team owns a backlog for its slice of value, has its own sprint rhythm, and collaborates with a shared architecture team for standards and guardrails. They hold a weekly integration review to ensure their work aligns, with a shared definition of done for every feature. Case 2 shows value streams in a larger program. The company maps three value streams: core product delivery, platform services, and customer support innovations. Leaders assign cross-cutting roles to align roadmaps, use a program board to track progress, and host quarterly showcases to celebrate cross-stream wins. Communities of practice run monthly sessions where teams share testing patterns and accessibility improvements, ensuring new features meet broad standards without slowing delivery.

Common pitfalls here include over-architecting the structure, which can create confusion and slow teams down; under-structuring, which can leave teams without enough guidance to act. Quick fixes are to pilot one or two feature teams first and test the value-stream idea with a single, clear outcome. If a community of practice stagnates, rotate facilitators and set a rolling topic list to keep conversations practical and relevant.

Key takeaway: Scale with a balanced mix of end-to-end feature ownership, end-to-end value mapping, and shared learning communities that spread best practices without overloading teams.

Ensuring alignment, governance, and program-level flow

As you scale, you must keep alignment with the big-picture outcomes while letting teams operate with enough autonomy to move fast. Alignment creates coherence; governance provides guardrails; program-level flow keeps everything moving in a synchronized cadence.

Step 1: Agree on top-level outcomes and measurable goals. Translate strategic aims into concrete, observable targets that teams can influence directly. Use simple metrics that reflect customer value, such as time-to-delivery, quality indicators, and customer impact, rather than just internal process metrics. Rationale: when teams see how their work ties to meaningful outcomes, motivation and focus rise.

Step 2: Establish lightweight governance and decision rights. Decide who makes what kind of decisions, when escalation is needed, and how conflicts are resolved. Keep it light enough to avoid bottlenecks but clear enough to prevent drift. Rationale: good governance removes ambiguity and keeps decisions timely.

Step 3: Implement program-level flow with a visible backlog and cadence. Create a program backlog that aggregates work across teams and aligns with the value streams. Use a program board or similar artifact to show progress, dependencies, and risks at a glance. Rationale: a shared flow picture helps all teams stay synchronized and helps leaders see where to intervene.

Step 4: Regular reviews, risk checks, and adjustment points. Schedule frequent, short reviews that focus on progress toward outcomes, readiness for upcoming milestones, and any emerging risks. Allow teams to adjust plans in response to new information rather than sticking to a rigid script. Rationale: adaptive planning keeps momentum and reduces waste.

Case examples illustrate how alignment and governance play out in real settings. Case 3 involves a growing platform where executives set broad outcomes, while product teams execute on those outcomes within a shared program backlog. The governance group keeps tension between speed and safety by approving critical changes and moderating scope when necessary. Case 4 shows a cross-functional program where the program board meets monthly to review progress, resolve escalations, and re-prioritize work across value streams. The alignment practice helps everyone stay focused on customer outcomes even as teams experiment and learn.

From time to time you'll encounter common obstacles. Conflicting priorities between teams, unclear ownership of outcomes, or a backlog that grows unwieldy are all signals to pause, simplify, and realign. Quick fixes include clarifying the top three outcomes for the program, reconciling backlog items into one visible list, and resetting the governance cadence to ensure timely decision-making. The aim is not to crush creativity but to channel it toward shared goals with minimal friction.

Key takeaway: Clear outcomes, light governance, and a transparent program flow create a predictable path for teams to deliver value together.

Coming up next Subtittle: Tools, Automation, and Effective Workflows

1) Choosing boards, backlog tools, and CI/CD integrations wisely,

2) Automating repetitive processes to reduce manual handoffs,

3) Designing workflows that support distributed and hybrid teams

Chapter 9

Tools, Automation, and Effective Workflows

By the end of this chapter, you will be able to choose boards, backlog tools, and CI/CD integrations wisely; automate repetitive processes to reduce manual handoffs; and design workflows that support distributed and hybrid teams.

Choosing boards, backlog tools, and CI/CD integrations wisely

Step 1. Clarify your team's work and constraints. Identify how many people you have, where they are located, and what kind of work you do. Note whether you need strict traceability, fast iteration, or strong visual signals. The clearer your setup, the easier it is to pick tools that fit without forcing you into a rigid process.

Step 2. List must-have features for each tool category. For boards, look for visibility (filters, swimlanes), ease of use, and quick status updates. For backlog tools, seek clear prioritization, grooming support, and links to work items. For CI/CD, check how easily you can trigger builds from work items, automate tests, and deploy safely. If something feels shoehorned, it's a red flag you'll fight later.

Step 3. Create a simple comparison matrix. Put a handful of popular options side by side and rate them on three axes: usability, integration capability, and cost. Don't chase every feature—focus on what your team will actually use. Small differences can compound into big time savings or headaches.

Step 4. Verify integrations with your current stack. Confirm that the board supports your source control, testing tools, and deployment steps. Two-way syncing is ideal so work moves smoothly between planning and delivery, and so people aren't duplicating work in two places.

Step 5. Run a low-risk pilot. Pick a small project, set up a board, a backlog, and a CI/CD trigger. Observe how work items flow, how decisions are recorded, and whether the automation reduces friction. Collect quick feedback from the team and adjust before you roll out widely.

Examples and micro-cases

Example A. A small remote team uses a lightweight board with simple backlogs and a straightforward CI workflow. They connect the board to their version control so creating or updating a task mirrors a commit or pull request. When a task moves to code review, the board automatically updates its status, and the deployment pipeline is triggered only when the code passes tests. The team enjoys clear visibility without heavy administration, and standups stay focused on value.

Example B. A mid-sized team uses a robust board with advanced filters and swimlanes. They pair it with a formal backlog that periodically refines priorities and links each item to a test or deployment step. Their CI/CD setup runs nightly builds and automatic checks on merged code, with dashboards that show build health, test pass rates, and release readiness. They report faster feedback and fewer manual handoffs because the links between planning, testing, and deploying stay tight.

Automating repetitive processes to reduce manual handoffs

Step 1. Map the repetitive tasks that slow you down. List things like status updates, manual data entry, duplicate reporting, and manual handoffs between teams. The goal is to see where you can gain time back without sacrificing accuracy.

Step 2. Prioritize automation candidates by impact and effort. Start with high-impact, low-effort tasks—things that save the most time with a small amount of setup. Move more complex automations later as you build confidence and reliability.

Step 3. Choose automation approaches that fit your tools. Use built-in automation features in your boards or CI/CD platforms when they exist. If not, consider small scripts or simple automation tools that run in your environment. Keep it simple enough that when someone new joins, they can understand how it works quickly.

Step 4. Build automation with safeguards. Add clear failure alerts, manual override options, and a rollback path. Document what the automation does in plain language so teammates can review it, test it, and trust it.

Step 5. Pilot with one repeatable process and measure results. Track time saved, error reductions, and any new bottlenecks. If the automation introduces new failures or complexity, adjust or revert before expanding.

Step 6. Expand cautiously. After you prove a few automations, extend the approach to neighboring tasks. Use a light-change protocol: small, reversible changes with quick reviews.

Step 7. Create a living automation log. Record what you automated, why, who approved it, and how to troubleshoot. This helps when people rotate roles or when you need to audit the workflow.

Step 8. Foster a culture of continuous improvement. Encourage teammates to propose automations and run quick experiments. Celebrate wins and learn from near-misses.

Step 9. Establish ownership and maintenance routines. Assign a person or small team to monitor each automation, check for drift, and refresh documentation as needed.

Step 10. Define metrics to track automation success. Use simple measures: time saved per task, error rate after automation, and user satisfaction with the new flow.

Step 11. Safeguard security and compliance. Ensure that automations don't reveal sensitive data or bypass required approvals. Use access controls and review steps where appropriate.

Step 12. Prepare for scale. As you automate more, you'll need a governance model so new automations don't collide. Create a lightweight intake process for automation requests.

Step 13. Keep dependencies clear. If an automation relies on a third-party service, document the service's status, reliability, and contingency plans.

Step 14. Test in a non-production environment when possible. If your tools allow it, run automations against a copy of real data to catch issues without affecting live work.

Step 15. Teach the team how to use what you've built. Create a quick, friendly guide and offer short demos so everyone understands the benefits and how to recover if something goes wrong.

Step 16. Monitor and adjust based on feedback. Schedule regular check-ins to assess whether automations still meet needs as teams evolve.

Step 17. Build in user-friendly controls. Where possible, offer simple on/off toggles and manual overrides so people can intervene when automation isn't quite right.

Step 18. Document failures and lessons learned. When something breaks, write down what happened and how you fixed it to prevent the same issue from reoccurring.

Step 19. Create a rollback plan. If an automation causes trouble, you should be able to disable it quickly and revert to the old process with minimal disruption.

Step 20. Align automations with sprint rhythms. Time automations to support planning and review cycles, not just code delivery, so teams feel the improvements.

Step 21. Build a sequencing plan. Don't automate everything at once. Prioritize a pipeline of automations so you can learn and adjust in steps.

Step 22. Seek feedback from all roles. Talk to developers, testers, product owners, and operations to gather diverse perspectives on what works and what doesn't.

Step 23. Celebrate small wins publicly. A quick acknowledgment helps sustain momentum and shows automation pays off.

Step 24. Keep the human in the loop. Automations should speed work, not remove essential human judgment. Leave key decision points, reviews, and problem-solving to people.

Designing workflows that support distributed and hybrid teams

Step 1. Map current workflows across locations. Draw a clear picture of who does what, when, and where. Identify bottlenecks caused by distance, time zones, or uneven access to information.

Step 2. Design for asynchronous collaboration. Favor written updates, shared documents, and records that teammates can access anytime. Use clear handoffs and well-defined inputs/outputs for each step.

Step 3. Create lean ceremonies with practical outcomes. Make meetings purposeful, timeboxed, and action-focused. Use concise agendas and keep minutes to a shared, searchable place so everyone can catch up later.

Step 4. Clarify roles and responsibilities. Define who makes decisions, who provides input, and who signs off on progress. Written ownership reduces confusion and speeds progress.

Step 5. Establish explicit SLAs and response times. For example, define when backlog items should be reviewed, when updates must appear in the board, and how quickly feedback is expected after a stand-up.

Step 6. Build robust documentation culture. Maintain living documents for processes, rules, and definitions of done. Easy-to-find documentation reduces delays when people join or switch roles.

Step 7. Use collaboration tools with clear visibility. Choose tools that show real-time status and recent changes, but also keep a reliable history so anyone can audit what happened and why.

Step 8. Align handoffs to natural work boundaries. Reduce cross-team handoffs by aligning responsibilities with how work actually flows, not just how teams are structured.

Step 9. Schedule reliable cadence for distributed teams. Pick a rhythm that works across time zones—perhaps a core overlap window for live meetings and asynchronous updates outside that window.

Step 10. Create a shared mental model. Connect goals, constraints, and success measures so everyone understands the same big picture, even if they sit in different places.

Step 11. Build rituals that respect time zones. For remote or hybrid teams, design rituals that don't demand everyone be present at odd hours. Use asynchronous summaries to keep everyone informed.

Step 12. Prioritize accessibility and inclusivity. Ensure documents, boards, and workflows are easy to read, with clear language and accessible formats so every team member can participate.

Step 13. Integrate feedback loops into the flow. Regularly collect quick feedback after major milestones and adjust the workflow. Small, frequent adjustments beat big overhauls.

Step 14. Test changes in a safe environment. Try a new workflow on a single project or a single team before expanding, so you can learn without risking the whole program.

Step 15. Create a change-management plan. When you adjust workflows, plan how you'll communicate, train, and support teams to adopt the change smoothly.

Step 16. Establish a documentation routine. Schedule short, regular updates to reflect new ways of working, ensuring that the knowledge stays current.

Step 17. Align performance metrics with workflow goals. Track indicators like cycle time, lead time, and completion rate to verify that the workflow improvements are actually delivering faster value.

Step 18. Prepare for scaling across teams. As teams grow or reconfigure, ensure workflows can stretch to accommodate more work items, without becoming unwieldy.

Step 19. Build a distributed ownership model. Distribute responsibility for different parts of the workflow so no single person becomes a bottleneck.

Step 20. Foster trust and psychological safety. Encourage open discussion about what works and what doesn't. Safe voices lead to better, faster improvements.

Step 21. Use lightweight governance. Put just enough structure in place to keep things moving, without stifling creativity or slowing progress with rules.

Step 22. Invest in continuous learning. Offer quick trainings, micro-lessons, and buddy-system support so people stay competent with the evolving workflows.

Step 23. Prepare for contingencies. Plan for outages, tool failures, or sudden changes in staffing. Clear backup workflows help teams recover quickly.

Step 24. Review and refresh quarterly. Schedule a regular review to prune unnecessary steps, retire obsolete practices, and refresh tools to keep the system nimble.

Templates and tools to copy

- Tool Evaluation Checklist

  - Board usability: easy to learn, intuitive navigation

  - Backlog features: clear prioritization, grooming support

- CI/CD integration: triggers, automation hooks, reliability

- Security and permissions: access control, data protection

- Cost and maintenance: total cost, ease of scaling

- Learning curve and onboarding: time to get new users productive

- Automation Plan Template

- Problem: what repetitive task you want to automate

- Candidate tasks: list tasks to automate

- Expected impact: time saved, error reduction
- Implementation steps: how you'll implement
- Rollout plan: pilot, feedback, wider rollout
- Metrics: how you'll measure success
- Owners: who is responsible

- Workflow Map Template for Distributed Teams
  - Start state: current flow
  - End state: desired flow
  - Roles and responsibilities: who does what
  - Handoffs: where items move between teams

- Time windows: overlap and asynchronous work

- Documentation: where updates live

Exercises

Exercise 1. Tool inventory audit. Spend 15 minutes listing all boards, backlog tools, and CI/CD integrations in use. Outcome: a one-page map of current tools and how they connect.

Exercise 2. Feature fit check. For each tool, rate on usability, integration, and cost from 1 to 5. Outcome: a short scorecard to guide choices.

Exercise 3. Quick integration test. Pick a small task and connect it across board, backlog, and CI/CD. Outcome: a visible, verifiable connection from planning to delivery.

Exercise 4. Pilot project kickoff. Start a tiny project with a board, backlog, and automation in place. Outcome: a baseline for what works and what doesn't.

Exercise 5. Automation candidate list. List five repetitive tasks suitable for automation and mark ease of implementation. Outcome: a ready queue for automation work.

Exercise 6. Risk assessment for automation. Note potential failure points and how you'll mitigate them. Outcome: a safety plan.

Exercise 7. Authorization and access review. Check who has access to boards, backlogs, and automation tools. Outcome: appropriate permissions for everyone.

Exercise 8. Documentation audit. Review where the workflow and automations are documented. Outcome: a single source of truth that's easy to find.

Exercise 9. Performance metrics setup. Choose two metrics to track automation impact (time saved, error rate). Outcome: a measurement plan.

Exercise 10. Change-management plan. Draft a simple plan for introducing a workflow change to the team. Outcome: a smooth rollout approach.

Exercise 11. Stakeholder check-in. Schedule 10 minutes for a quick feedback loop with each major user group. Outcome: early signals on acceptance.

Exercise 12. Accessibility check. Review boards and docs for readability and accessibility. Outcome: everyone can participate comfortably.

Exercise 13. Asynchronous ceremony design. Create a plan for a leaning, non-overlapping stand-up and review cadence. Outcome: clear expectations for remote participants.

Exercise 14. Handoff clarity test. Walk through a typical handoff and make sure inputs/outputs are explicit. Outcome: fewer miscommunications.

Exercise 15. Version control for workflows. Maintain a changelog of workflow updates. Outcome: traceable evolution of practices.

Exercise 16. Rehearsal for outages. Run a small drill to simulate an automation failure and recovery. Outcome: rapid response readiness.

Exercise 17. Training bite-size session. Prepare a 20-minute lesson for new joiners on the workflow. Outcome: faster onboarding.

Exercise 18. Knowledge-sharing moment. Schedule a monthly 15-minute session where team members share tips about the tools. Outcome: continuous learning.

Exercise 19. SLA clarity check. Review agreed response times and update them if needed. Outcome: realistic expectations.

Exercise 20. Dependency mapping. List external services your automations rely on and note contingency plans. Outcome: better resilience.

Exercise 21. Quarterly workflow review. Run a mini-review of the workflow to prune or adjust. Outcome: lean, effective processes.

Exercise 22. Cross-team alignment meeting. Bring teams together to confirm shared goals and flow. Outcome: stronger collaboration.

Exercise 23. Documentation refresh sprint. Dedicate a sprint to refreshing docs and templates. Outcome: up-to-date guidance.

Exercise 24. Celebration of learning. Acknowledge improvements and lessons learned publicly. Outcome: motivation and morale boost.

Troubleshooting

- Problem: A board item doesn't update when code changes.

Quick fix: verify the integration trigger is configured correctly and the mapping between work item status and code events is accurate.

- Problem: An automation runs but creates duplicate work.

Quick fix: add idempotent checks so the automation can run safely without repeating the same action.

- Problem: A task moves to done but isn't reflected in reports.

Quick fix: confirm that all reporting feeds refresh on a schedule and that the data source is correct.

- Problem: Team members disagree about how a workflow should operate.

Quick fix: run a short, closed-loop experiment with a single change, document results, and solicit structured feedback before wider adoption.

- Problem: Access to tools is uneven across locations.

Quick fix: review permissions, ensure role-based access, and set up a shared, accessible onboarding guide.

Coming up next Subtittle: Growing Your Coaching Practice

1) Building a personal development plan and learning routines,

2) Seeking supervision, peer coaching, and reflective feedback,

3) Maintaining professional ethics, credibility, and resilience

Key Takeaway: Well-chosen boards, smooth automation, and clear, inclusive workflows reduce friction so teams can focus on delivering value.

Transition: With solid tools, reliable automation, and well-designed workflows in place, you're ready to deepen your coaching practice. In the next chapter, you'll learn how to grow your coaching skills, seek guidance, and build a practice that stays ethical, credible, and resilient.

Chapter 10

Growing Your Coaching Practice

By the end of this chapter, you will have a practical plan to grow your coaching practice, reliable sources of feedback, and a durable ethical framework you can count on every day.

Building a personal development plan and learning routines

Your development as a coach starts with a simple map: what you want to improve, how you will learn it, and how you will practice it in real situations. A personal development plan (PDP) is not a long, complicated document. It's a concise guide that keeps you focused and moving forward. Think of it as a small GPS for your coaching journey.

First, clarify your coaching goals. Ask yourself what you want to get better at in the next three to six months. Do you want to improve your listening with teams? Get better at asking provocative questions? Help teams make faster, clearer decisions? Write down two to four concrete goals. Make them specific, observable, and testable. For example: "Improve the clarity of sprint goals by asking two follow-up questions in every planning session," or "Facilitate two retrospectives that end with a defined experiment and a measurable outcome."

Next, design your learning routine. A routine is a lightweight, repeatable set of activities you actually do. It should fit into your life, not add a heavy load. A practical plan might look like this:

- Short reading: 20–30 minutes, three times per week, focusing on one concept (listening techniques, feedback models, or facilitation tips).

- Mini practice: 15–20 minutes, twice a week, practicing one skill with a friend, mentor, or even with a simulated team.

- Real-world application: apply what you've learned in one real coaching moment each week and note what happened.

- Review and reflect: 10–15 minutes after each coaching session to capture what worked and what didn't.

In my experience, small, consistent steps beat big, sporadic efforts. You don't need to master everything at once. Build a pocket of dependable skills, then add more as you go.

Now add a deliberate-practice habit. Deliberate practice is not just "doing more." It's practicing with intent, getting feedback, and making tiny adjustments. Pick one skill to improve per month, practice it in low-risk settings (a practice session with peers, a volunteer role, or a simulated team), and then check what changed in real coaching work. The goal is to move from being able to do something to doing it with ease and consistency.

Create a small library of trusted resources. The point isn't to read everything but to collect a few reliable sources you return to. Select short, practical guides, video tutorials, or articles that explain a technique in clear terms. Keep a simple note file where you summarize the most useful ideas in your own words. When you're stuck, you can review your notes and choose one actionable tactic to try.

Set a monthly reflection and adjustment moment. At the end of every month, review your PDP. Did you move toward your goals? Which routines kept you on track? Which habits slipped, and why? Use this time to adjust your goals, refresh your learning plan, and reset your calendar. This keeps your plan alive and useful, not a paper trophy you admire but never use.

Two micro-cases to illustrate this point:

- Case A: Mia, a high school student who helps teammates prepare for class projects, creates a PDP focused on listening and asking clarifying questions. She sets a goal to reduce misunderstandings by 40% in group work within two months. Her routine includes 20 minutes of reading on active listening twice a week and a 15-minute practice session with a friend where she reframes questions for better clarity. After six weeks, she notes fewer repeated questions in group tasks and feels more confident guiding discussions.

- Case B: Sam, a community volunteer who coaches a youth robotics team, builds a PDP around facilitating efficient stand-ups and experiments. He schedules one micro-lesson per week, records a short video of a planning session, and asks a mentor for feedback. He discovers that short, precise updates lead to clearer weekly plans, and his team starts trying a small experiment each sprint rather than debating big topics for hours.

Common pitfalls and quick fixes

- Too ambitious goals: Start with two goals you can actually move on in eight weeks. If you bite off more than you can chew, you'll stall. Fix: scale back to one main goal and one supporting skill.

- Inconsistent routines: Life is busy; routines slip. Fix: set fixed times on your calendar, link them to existing habits (after school, before dinner), and keep the session short but regular.

- No easy feedback loop: Without feedback, you won't know what to adjust. Fix: ask for quick, specific feedback after each coaching moment, and note it in your PDP.

Exercises for Building Your PDP and Routine (2–4 quick tasks, each with timing and check progress)

- Exercise 1: Draft your PDP (60 minutes). Write two to four coaching goals you want to reach in the next three months. For each goal, add one clear measurable outcome and one small action you will take this week to move toward it. Check progress after four weeks by asking yourself if the goal feels closer to done and what evidence changed.

- Exercise 2: Design your learning routine (30 minutes). Choose two learning activities (for example, one short article and one practice session with a peer) and schedule them for the next four weeks. Track whether you actually did them and what you learned after each week.

- Exercise 3: Start a tiny practice journal (15 minutes per week). After every coaching moment, write one paragraph about what you learned, what surprised you, and what you will change next time.

- Exercise 4: Build a mini-resource list (20 minutes). Collect three reliable sources on a technique you want to improve, summarize the key idea in a sentence or two, and save it in your learning folder for quick review.

Tools and templates you can copy

- Personal Development Plan (PDP) snapshot:

Goals:

Outcomes you want to see:

One action per week you will take to move toward the goal:

Learning routine (days and times):

Review date:

- Quick feedback checklist: After a coaching moment, answer these three questions: What happened? What was effective? What will I adjust next time?

- Practice journal template: Date, Situation, Skill practiced, What worked, What didn't, Next step.

Seeking supervision, peer coaching, and reflective feedback

Supervision is a guided space where you discuss coaching moments with a more experienced mentor. Peer coaching is when you coach and are coached by someone at a similar level. Reflective feedback is your own practice of looking back honestly at what happened, why it happened, and how you can get better next time. All three are essential for growing confidence and competence.

Start by finding someone you trust and respect. Look for a supervisor or mentor who has real-world coaching experience, preferably with teams that resemble the ones you work with. If you're in school or a local club, ask a teacher, coach, or experienced facilitator if they would supervise you for a few sessions. Agree on a schedule that fits both of you, such as one 60-minute session each month, plus a quick check-in mid-month.

Structure your supervision or coaching conversations around recent coaching experiences. Bring one or two concrete moments, describe what you tried, and share your outcomes. Ask for three kinds of input: what you did well, what you could do more effectively, and what you should try next time. The goal is not to please the mentor but to learn from the real work you're doing.

Engage in peer coaching as a regular practice. Pair up with a fellow beginner or near-peer who shares your learning goals. Use a simple structure:

observe one coaching moment, give a short, targeted feedback, then switch roles. Repeat with a different moment. The aim is to build a safe, collaborative loop where both of you grow.

Reflection is your ongoing practice of turning experience into learning. After each coaching moment, write or speak a short reflection. Include what happened, what you learned, and what you'll try next time. Over time, your reflections become a personal playbook you can return to when you're stuck.

Two micro-cases for supervision and peer coaching

- Case A: Lina, a middle school tutor who coaches a group project, sets up monthly supervision with a local teacher. She brings two tricky moments: a plan that kept dragging and a conflict among team members. Her supervisor suggests reframing questions to surface assumptions and to test ideas with a quick experiment. Lina leaves with a concrete plan to run a one-question experiment at the start of the next planning session.

- Case B: Noah, a club leader who mentors younger students in building a science fair project, pairs with a peer coach. They shadow one planning session, then discuss what happened, share one technique to improve listening, and try it in the next meeting. After four weeks, they both notice more focus, fewer side conversations, and clearer action steps.

Common pitfalls and quick fixes

- Avoiding feedback: People fear criticism, but feedback is essential. Fix: schedule regular feedback moments and treat them as a normal part of practice, not a judgment.

- One-way feedback: Feedback should be a two-way street. Fix: invite your supervisee to critique your coaching and to suggest one improvement you should try next time.

- Skipping supervision when busy: Busy times tempt you to skip. Fix: protect the supervision slot as a non-negotiable commitment; the payoff is shorter learning cycles when things get hard.

Exercises for Supervision, Peer Coaching, and Reflective Feedback (2–4 tasks)

- Exercise 1: Schedule supervision and prepare (30 minutes). Reach out to a potential supervisor, agree on a time, and write down two moments you want to discuss.

- Exercise 2: Start a peer-coaching duo (30 minutes). Pair with a peer, agree on a structure (one coaching moment per week for four weeks), and pick a resting point to reflect on progress after four sessions.

- Exercise 3: Create a reflection ritual (15 minutes per week). After each coaching moment, record one strength, one area to improve, and one experiment you'll try next time.

Tools and templates you can copy

- Supervision preparation sheet: date, coaching moment, goals for the session, questions for the supervisor, notes from the discussion.

- Peer coaching protocol: partner name, session date, moment observed, feedback given, next steps, date for the next session.

- Reflective minus-one template: what happened, why it happened, what you learned, what you'll change next time.

Maintaining professional ethics, credibility, and resilience

Ethics are the rules that protect everyone involved in coaching. They include honesty, confidentiality, respect, fairness, and consent. You don't need fancy codes to be ethical; you just need to act in a way that shows care for others and keeps things safe and respectful. Protect people's privacy, share only information that is appropriate, and never use coaching moments to gain unfair advantage for yourself.

Credibility is earned through consistent action, reliability, and clear results. Be dependable: show up on time, follow through on what you say you will do, and be transparent about what you can and cannot help with. Document your coaching moments, so you have a record of what you tried, what happened, and what you learned. This creates a track record that people can trust.

Resilience is the ability to keep going when things don't go as planned. Setbacks happen in every coaching journey: teams get stuck, plans change, emotions rise, and progress can feel slow. Build resilience by practicing self-care, keeping a supportive circle, and using setbacks as data. Ask yourself: What did this teach me? What will I try differently next time? What is one small action I can take today to move forward?

Two micro-cases for ethics, credibility, and resilience

- Case A: A high school coach learns that a team's private conversation should stay private. They explain boundaries clearly and obtain consent before sharing anything with mentors. This builds trust and avoids unintentional harm.

- Case B: A junior coach faces a late delivery on a project and admits the mistake openly, apologizes, and creates a quick plan to recover. The team sees responsibility in action, not blame, and morale stays high.

Common pitfalls and quick fixes

- Breaches of confidentiality: Do not disclose names or sensitive details outside the team without permission. Fix: keep notes generic and anonymized when sharing with mentors.

- Inconsistency in behavior: If actions don't match words, trust erodes. Fix: document commitments and review them weekly.

- Burnout and overreach: Trying to do too much can hurt ethics and credibility. Fix: set limits, ask for help, and prioritize essential coaching moments over busywork.

Exercises for Ethics, Credibility, and Resilience (2–4 tasks)

- Exercise 1: Write a brief ethics pledge (20 minutes). List three commitments you will keep in every coaching moment (privacy, respect, consent). Review it monthly.

- Exercise 2: Build a credibility log (15 minutes per week). Record one coaching moment where you did something well and one where you could improve, plus a plan to close the gap.

- Exercise 3: Create a resilience plan (20 minutes). Identify two self-care practices you will use during stressful weeks and schedule them in your calendar.

Tools and templates you can copy

- Ethics pledge template: I commit to [principle], I will [action], I will [how to handle a challenge].

- Credibility log template: Date, Coaching moment, What went well, What to improve, Next action.

- Resilience plan template: Practice, Time, Trigger, Expected benefit, Check-in date.

Key Takeaway: A steady practice of personal development, guided feedback, and strong ethics builds a coaching habit that lasts and grows with you.

Transition: With a solid habit of continuous learning, thoughtful supervision, and unwavering ethics, you're ready to apply these foundations to the next layer of agile work—how to connect coaching with the actual frameworks and practices teams use every day. In the next chapter, you'll explore Core Agile Frameworks and Practices and learn how to bring your growing coaching maturity into Scrum, Kanban, and beyond.

Dear Reader,

Thank you for exploring this series focused on failures and the power of comeback stories. If you find value in these stories and believe in the importance of embracing setbacks as part of growth, we appreciate your support. Please consider sharing a positive review on the platform where you accessed this series.

Your feedback helps spread the message, inspiring more young readers to see challenges as opportunities and to believe in their potential. We understand that mistakes happen, and we thank you for your understanding.

www.ingramcontent.com/pod-product-compliance
Lightning Source LLC
LaVergne TN
LVHW020233210926
848481LV00016B/1824